Not Yo Mama's Emily Post:
A Guide to Etiquette in an Online World

Minute Help Guides

Minute Help Press
www.minutehelp.com

© 2011. All Rights Reserved.

Table of Contents

INTRODUCTION 3

CHAPTER 1: ETIQUETTE IN CONVERSATION...5

TOPIC HIJACKER 6

LOOKING AT YOUR PHONE..6

KNOW YOUR AUDIENCE 7

THE TOPPER...7

YOUR ROYAL MAJESTY 8

F&%# SH#& 9

WHAT TIME IS IT?..9

THE OTHER GUYS...9

ONE-SIDED CONVERSATION 10

INTERRUPTING 10

CHAPTER 2: BUSINESS ETIQUETTE 11

MULTICULTURAL ETIQUETTE 12

CHAPTER 3: CELL PHONE ETIQUETTE 13

TEXTING ETIQUETTE 18

CHAPTER 4: EMAIL ETIQUETTE...........................21

CHAPTER 5: INSTANT MESSAGING (IM) ETIQUETTE 26

CHAPTER 6: FACEBOOK ETIQUETTE...................30

CHAPTER 7: YOUTUBE ETIQUETTE......................42

CHAPTER 8: TWITTER ETIQUETTE 46

CHAPTER 9: EBAY FEEDBACK ETIQUETTE.......51

Introduction

Etiquette is defined as, "a code of behavior that delineates expectations for social behavior according to contemporary conventional norms within a society, social class, or group. The French word étiquette, literally signifying a tag or label, first appeared in English around 1750."

Etiquette is an important aspect of society at large and plays a large role in an individual's success or failure. Although the definition above is very clear, it can be elusive to define because of the various frameworks it fits into. For example, we are all familiar with what a car is, but there are literally thousands of different makes and models.

Etiquette is similar because everyone knows what it is, but there are different versions of it. For example, there's online etiquette, in-person etiquette, email etiquette, and social media etiquette. And that's where we come in. We've developed this etiquette guide as a way to help people understand what types of behaviors are deemed acceptable in a variety of situations. Enjoy!

Chapter 1: Etiquette in Conversation

General social etiquette used in conversations hasn't changed much over the years. The discourse and language may have, but the same principles of good conversation etiquette still apply like they did 50 years ago.

Conversation isn't about being the best speaker who uses the biggest words. It's really all about having proper manners. It's about being polite and being aware of your audience and setting. For example, you probably wouldn't want to start sharing about all of your wild and crazy sex, drugs, and rock n' roll stories at church, or how your marriage failed miserably after six months while at a wedding.

There are different etiquette do's and don'ts depending on your audience and location, but we'll delve into that later. First off let's discuss some general conversation etiquette rules that will help you no matter what the occasion.

Topic Hijacker

Generally, everyone likes to talk about what suits them - work, sports, Hollywood gossip, etc. One of the biggest etiquette no-no's is to constantly change the conversation to what you want to talk about. It should be done in a natural way without you trying to sound like a telemarketer or used car salesman. It's pretty evident to the other person when they've just been railroaded into another topic. It's quite rude. Let the conversation flow naturally and transition from topic to topic.

Looking at your Phone

Wives and girlfriends everywhere can relate to this. You're trying to have a deep conversation with you man and he can't take his eyes off his phone. Technology is great, but constantly checking your phone or looking down at it while someone is talking to you signals that you really don't care what they are saying to you. It probably stems more from your phone and technology addiction, but it comes off as insulting. I'm sure the Fruit Ninja or Angry Birds can wait a few minutes until your conversation is over.

Know Your Audience

As was mentioned in the beginning of this section, it is quite important that you recognize your audience. Some people feel that they "shouldn't change for anyone, and what they see is what they get." That's fine if you want to be one of those people, but anyone with tact knows that you can highlight the diversity of your personality and conversation while remaining true to yourself at all times. Just be aware of the people you are talking to and adjust accordingly.

The Topper

No, this isn't what goes on top of a cake. The Topper is known as the person who always has to one up everyone in a conversation. If someone is talking about how they saw Coldplay in concert, the Topper will immediately talk about how they went to a Coldplay concert too, but also hung out with the band backstage and went to the after party. Toppers can never let someone else have the conversational spotlight. They have to be the star. This is a sure fire way to be alienated. Sure there are times when you should share great experiences, but not at the expense of others. Other people have the right to share exciting news about a new promotion or a cool experience without The Topper coming in to steal their thunder.

Your Royal Majesty

This conversation misstep happens frequently. A friend comes by and you're sitting down somewhere. They greet you politely and you sit there like royalty stuck to the throne. It's best to get up and greet them with a handshake or whatever pleasantry is appropriate. It's very disrespectful to stay seated.

F&%# Sh#&

Society has gotten a lot looser about cursing, but it's still best to err on the side of caution. We all drop the occasional f-bomb now and again, but a conversation shouldn't sound like a gangster rap song. There's just too big of a downside compared to upside with cursing. Even if everyone else talks like a sailor you should keep your tongue tamed.

What Time is It?

Again, this is similar to the technology faux pas. When someone is talking to you and you check your watch it signals to them that you're thinking, "God I wish I could get out of here. I'm too busy to listen to this fool speak right now." If you have to, keep your hands in your pocket.

The Other Guys

It's important to introduce the other people around you if you are speaking to someone else. It's pretty bad to leave the other person hanging helplessly in the conversation without introducing them.

One-Sided Conversation

The only one that enjoys the one-sided conversation is the person talking. Monopoly is a game – not a conversation technique.

Interrupting

We've all done it time and again. Sometimes it's even necessary if someone is monopolizing the conversation. But most of the time let the person say what they have to say before you interject.

Now that we've established the Ten Conversation Commandments, let's look briefly at some situational etiquette examples.

Chapter 2: Business Etiquette

While at a business luncheon you should highlight the professional side of yourself. If you are at a business luncheon or dinner and you are running late, even by a few minutes, you should call and let one of the guests know. Upon arriving you should apologize and state the reason if it is legitimate.

Never place your briefcase, bag, or electronics on the table. When you are seated, gently unfold the napkin and place it in your lap. And just like your mama taught you, do not eat until everyone gets their meal. Here are some other general do's and don'ts:

- Turn your phone to vibrate
- Use good posture
- Keep your elbows off the table
- Don't hold utensils in a fist
- Turn your head from the table if you have to sneeze
- Pre-arrange how the bill should be paid
- Don't talk with utensils in your hand

Multicultural Etiquette

Proper cultural etiquette is becoming more prevalent. There's no way one can know all of the proper etiquette from every culture, but here are a few pointers and facts to remember:

Long periods of silence are deemed comfortable and polite parts of communication in India and Japan, but are considered awkward in North America.

In Western culture it is polite to look the person in the eye when communicating. In Asia it is considered aggressive behavior. It is a sign of respect to look down at the floor with an elder while they are speaking.

A thumb's up sign is considered to mean all is well in many countries, but in many Islamic countries it is an offensive sexual gesture.

In business communication it is rude to exchange business cards at the beginning of a meeting in Asian countries. It is best to wait until the end of the meeting.

Chapter 3: Cell Phone Etiquette

Cell phones are carried by over 90% of adults. That means there's a whole lot of communication going on. With that said, there are certain etiquette guidelines when it comes to talking on the cell phone, as well as conversations that are better said in person. Here are some guidelines for cell phone etiquette.

Do not interrupt an in-person conversation for a cell phone conversation

The person standing in front of you always takes precedence over the person trying to call you on the cell phone. Of course there are exceptions to every rule. If it's your babysitter calling or you are expecting an important phone call politely excuse yourself and explain this to the person you are talking to.

When indoors watch tone, volume and language

There's nothing more annoying than being forced to hear every word of someone's cell phone conversation because they are so loud. When you are indoors be cognizant that there are others around who do not wish to hear every single word you are saying. Use your "indoor voice" when speaking on a cell phone in an indoor location. A good rule of thumb is to be at least ten feet from the nearest person when speaking on your phone indoors. If you have to talk loudly because of bad reception then it's best to go outside. Here are some places where it's best to not use your cell phone at all:

- Houses of worship/Temples
- Movie theaters
- Meetings
- Presentations
- Classrooms
- Libraries
- Airplanes

Avoid personal topics when others can hear

This is for your sake and the others who are within earshot. No one really wants to hear you describing your bad bout on the toilet because of last night's trip to the buffet. They also do not want to hear about how you caught your boyfriend cheating on you with your best friend. Those types of conversations are left to the confines of your home or somewhere else that is private. You never know who is listening and you don't want to embarrass yourself.

Acknowledge cell phone latency

What's that mean, you ask? There's often a delay between when you talk and when the person hears what you've said. That can cause all kinds of drama from offending someone to constant interruptions and awkward silences. Just politely tell the person that there's a delay involved, that way both of you are aware.

What to do about a dropped call

The average person experiences 2-4 dropped calls every week. So what do you do when in mid conversation the call is lost? Do you call back? Do you wait for them to call back? Do you forget about it and go on with your day? The proper cell phone etiquette says that the person who dialed the phone call should be the one who calls the other person back – even if it is not their phone that dropped the call.

Don't talk and text while driving

Not only is this a huge cell phone etiquette faux pas, it's one of the most dangerous activities you can do behind the wheel. In fact, it's against the law in most states. Experts say that texting while driving is equivalent to having a blood alcohol level of over .08, which is the legal limit for drunk driving in most states. If you simply can't wait to text then pull off the road or into a parking lot to text. Otherwise just wait until you're done driving.

One of the biggest cell phone etiquette mishaps is conducting a conversation via text or cell phone that should be done in person. Here's a list of things that should take place in person:

- Breaking up

- Breaking some bad news to someone, like a death in the family (unless it's long distance)
- Asking someone out
- Saying "I love you" for the first time
- Announcing pregnancy
- Announcing divorce

There are also things that are okay to do over the phone, but not text:

- Calling in sick for work
- Saying happy birthday when it's a close friend or family
- Condolences about a loss of life or other tragedy

Another potentially awkward moment can occur when someone is on their cell phone and you need them to get off of it. For example, you're leading the business meeting and Joe is not even listening because he's engrossed in updating his status on Facebook on his phone. How do you tell Joe to knock it off?

The best way is to announce beforehand or have a sign hanging up that says cell phone use is not permitted. By doing this you avoid pinpointing an individual. Now this may not work for situations like a meeting, but it's great for classrooms, theaters, museums, etc. When someone is blatantly being rude by using their cell phone you can try to make eye contact with them first to see if they get the hint. If not, it's certainly fine to ask them politely to put their cell phone away because of reason x, y or z. It's all in the delivery. Make sure you're polite and non-confrontational. The vast majority of people will gladly hang up their phone.

Texting Etiquette

We touched on this briefly in the previous section, but texting definitely needs some in-depth discussion. The average person sends 42 texts per day. The average 15 year-old…5 million. Okay, maybe not that much, but texting is now a major way people communicate. The data is staggering. There are over 4.1 billion text messages sent every day throughout the world. Since it's a new medium of communication, many people are not aware of proper text etiquette or as some people call it – textiquette.

Texting is a service that augments in-person or phone conversations. It was never meant to replace all other forms of communication. With that said, text messages should be informal, short pieces of communication that are not too deep. They should also use proper spelling and grammar.

You should always consider your audience when texting. For example, you wouldn't go up to your boss and say, "hey bro, what's up wit you dawg?" So that means you should also avoid slang and unprofessional words and acronyms while texting. If you're running late to a meeting it's better to text, "Sorry, running five minutes late to the meeting", instead of "L8 2 MTG. B THR N 5". Huh? Another important detail to point out – Put your name at the beginning. If the person does not have your number they will not know who the message is from.

The same basic communication rules used for phone and face to face conversations apply when texting family members, friends, and work colleagues. When texting with work colleagues make sure you err on the side of professionalism. Remember, the one thing about texts is that they are permanent. Sending an unprofessional or inappropriate text message to a co-worker could end up costing you your job.

Some people think that because it's a text the rules don't apply on what time you can send a message. You wouldn't think of calling someone at 2:00 AM, so don't send a text either. Be aware of people's schedules before you send out a message.

Unless it's with your family members, leave the slang alone. You could probably get away with an "lol", but that's about it. Instead, try saying something like "haha." Also, be wary of sending a text message that is too long. Some people's phones may not be able to display the entire message in one screen like yours, which means they will receive the text message in ten different chunks – that makes it very difficult to understand what is going on. Also, if you have to type a message two feet long then it's probably better said over the phone. Most experts say that a message over 160 characters should be a phone call instead of a text message.

Let's review when to text or call:

When to call rather than text:

- Not coming into work because you're sick
- Have some sad or bad news
- Mad at a friend or family member
- A message that could be misunderstood via text
- Urgent meetings
- Time sensitive communication

Chapter 4: Email Etiquette

The thing about emails, texts, and social networking posts is that they are forever immortalized in cyberspace. With that said, you should tread very carefully when communicating with anyone when using these communication mediums. Email has been around for a long time, so you would think people would have a solid understanding of email etiquette, but there are people every day that get into hot water over breaking email etiquette rules. Let's take a look at email etiquette that will help you avoid mistakes while using this pervasive form of communication.

Short and Sweet

Emails should be short and to the point. If you want to get your message read then make sure it is short. Many people delete emails that are too long (over 300 words). Make your most important point first, and clearly state why you sent the email in the first place. It's just too much work for the recipient to wade through your email.

Keep multiple subjects to a minimum

If you have to talk about multiple subjects it is best to send more than one email. It's people's natural tendency to only remember one subject in an email. By discussing one message per email you will likely get a response and you'll be able to keep your messages shorter.

Format correctly

No one likes to read one big block of text. Email can be formatted in a reader-friendly way. That means your paragraphs should be no longer than 3-4 lines. People are likely to look past your email if they see one giant block of text staring them back in the face.

Proper grammar and spelling

Most email programs have spell checker. Use it. An email full of grammar and spelling problems not only makes the sender look unprofessional and uneducated, it can leave the email message open for misunderstanding.

Tone

Communication involves so much more than written words. The little nuances of person to person communication are not available in email so you have to be mindful of your tone. Sarcasm should be avoided as it gets lost in translation. For example, you might type, "Thanks for nothing" and be totally joking, but the person on the other end may take it literally.

Never use email to criticize
Email is great for compliments and praises of co-workers, friends, and family. It should not be used as a means to correct others. Chances are the message will offend the person because you did it in writing and did not even care enough to speak to them face to face or on the phone.

Jokes, chain letters, forwards, etc

We've all received those annoying chain letters about Microsoft giving away free money and other nonsense. These letters are 99% fake. Also, never forward email that is inappropriate, racist, of a sexual nature, or offensive. Remember, email is not anonymous. It can be tracked. If you're unsure of whether or not to send, ask yourself "Would I want this message displayed on the front page of the newspaper with my name attached to it?" If you answered no, then forget about sending it.

ALL CAPS

Writing in all caps is the equivalent of yelling at someone via email. Besides, it's also harder to read and spell check can't check it.

Re-read

We often type emails fast and add words that are useless and don't make sense. Because of this it is best to re-read your email before sending it out.

Subject Line

Never send an email to anyone, especially work colleagues, without a subject line. This will help them evaluate if it should be opened or not. If it doesn't have a subject line it will probably be sent to the trash.

Abuse of the URGENT or HIGH PRIORITY Flag

If every email you send is marked as urgent people are going to get annoyed. Plus, if you actually send one that is urgent it will not be taken seriously. It's like equivalent of *The Boy Who Cried Wolf.* Only use it when necessary.

Reply All

Many people use the reply all button way too much. That just accounts for added email that takes up space. Only reply to people who are expected to reply to the message.

Just as with cell phone conversation and texting, email should be used in its proper context. You should never email someone concerning the following:

- Ending a relationship
- Asking for marriage (you'd be surprised)

- Important financial matters that may contain sensitive information
- Sad or impactful news such as a death or accident
- Thanking people who attended an event of yours such as a wedding, graduation, etc. (Send a thank you card instead)
- Asking someone out on a date

Chapter 5: Instant Messaging (IM) Etiquette

Instant messaging used to be "the way" to communicate online with others. It has fallen off a bit since the advent of social networking sites became popular, but IM still has its place in online communication. Let's take a look at some rules of etiquette to follow when instant messaging.

Replying to Instant Messages

Replying should take no longer than 3-5 minutes. The great thing about IM'ing is that it's a synchronous form of communication. In other words, the communication between parties is occurring at the same time. It's live. Think of it this way; if someone asked you a question in a face-to-face or phone conversation, would you wait a few minutes before answering them? Of course not, because that would be considered rude. The same can be said for instant messaging. You should reply as quickly as possible or let the person know you have to end the chat session.

Avoid Sarcasm
This is a rule that applies to all forms of written communication. It's just too easy for the comment to be taken the wrong way. Instead, choose a more direct form of communication void of sarcastic comments.

Too many Acronyms
Even though you know what ROFL and PLOMSWT mean, a lot of people don't. Too many acronyms affect your message's ability to convey any sort of clear meaning. They are also hard to read. Unless you're a group of 15 year olds, avoid the overuse of acronyms.

Leaving your Computer
If you are planning on being away from your computer for longer than five minutes, type "be right back" or "BRB" to the person on the other end. Don't leave them hanging.

Font and Color
Fancy and light colored fonts are hard to read for recipients. Stick to black colored, plain font such as Arial, Times New Roman, and the like.

Consider your Audience
As with all forms of online communication, it is important to consider who you are talking to. When IM'ing your boss make sure to be very professional and responsive. Also, never speak badly about a co-worker or the organization while IM'ing with your boss or other co-workers.

When instant messaging with family and friends treat the conversation as you would any other time. Just remember that what you say is in writing, so be careful about speaking negative words about family members and friends because the person on the other end could end up sending that message to the person you were speaking negatively about.

Keep it Light

Instant messages are not meant to be long drawn out conversations that take place all night long. Keep the subject matter light and keep the conversations to a minimum. If you really want to talk about something deep, use the phone.

Private Information

One thing about online communication is that you do not know who you are talking to. It's bad etiquette, and very unsafe, to disclose personal information with someone during an IM session. Never ask someone for their personal information and never give your personal information via instant message.

Chapter 6: Facebook Etiquette

Facebook is easily the most visited website in the world. According to the Facebook website there are over 800 million active users. The social media website, founded in 2004 by Harvard student Mark Zuckerberg, has changed how people communicate and connect. Facebook's rapid rise to the top has not been without a few bumps.

Some people feel the platform is too invasive, and that people's privacy has been compromised. Others feel the site promotes surface friendships and has hampered intimate relationships. But despite all of the criticism, Facebook is a true global phenomenon that's here to stay.

Because of its widespread use there are certainly some etiquette practices that you should follow. Let's take a look:

The one thing about Facebook that you need to remember is that whatever you post on your "wall" can be seen by your entire network of friends and all of their friends. There have been many that have forgotten this fact and ended up losing their job, destroying their reputation, and damaging relationships. For example, a school administrator in Massachusetts making over $92,000 a year lost her job in just one day after she went on a rant posting negative comments about students and parents.

She was not schooled in the ways of Facebook and thought she was posting a private message to a friend. The comments were seen by some of the student's parents and caused an outrage in the community. The teacher was forced to resign that same day. That awful story leads us to Facebook etiquette lesson number one: Never use Facebook as a way to blow off steam.

As with email and other forms of electronic communication, Facebook wall posts and messages are permanent. If you need to vent about something use the phone, a private journal, or some other means. Even Facebook founder Mark Zuckerberg has gotten into hot water because of some disparaging emails he sent to friends about Facebook users during the site's early days.

Here are some other Facebook etiquette tips to follow:

If these walls could talk

At Facebook, the walls really do have ears – and eyes. That means you should be very mindful about what you post on your public Facebook wall. Photos of wild behavior have cost several people their jobs, and even students have lost the chance at getting into the college of their dreams. More and more organizations are using Facebook as a type of background checking tool, which means racy photos and controversial posts can get you into hot water. Remember, your Facebook page is an extension of your character. If you want to be known as a person of character and integrity then don't post rants about how you hate your boss or teachers, and forget about posting pics of last weekend's party.

You also want to be very careful about what you write in your status update. Updating your personal status with a generic statement may seem harmless, but you never know how someone in your social network may interpret it. That doesn't mean you have to consider every single word you type, but being mindful of what you post is a smart move. As was discussed in earlier sections of this guide, the newspaper test works well for Facebook too.

Don't vent about work

You wouldn't think of spray painting "I hate my boss" on the outside of your house because it could get you fired, right? Well, that's exactly what you are doing when you vent about work on your wall. Remember that Facebook is not a diary. It's a public platform that weaves people's lives together. That means you shouldn't write something that you don't want everyone to see. That includes venting about work. That's the fastest way to get a bad reputation on the job. It could also cost you your job.

Photo tagging

Facebook allows you to tag your friends in photos. Be mindful of tagging your friends in photos that may be less than endearing. For example, your friend Sara may not want to be tagged in the photo you took of her waking up in the morning. Be courteous about tagging and ask yourself "would I want to be tagged in this photo if I were this person?" If the answer is no – skip the photo tag.

Facebook profile picture

There are some people that believe that Facebook is for your personal life while other sites liked LinkedIn are for your professional life. Facebook can be whatever you want it to be. Most use it as a mixture of both personal and professional. With that said, it's best to err on the side of professional or neutral when choosing your profile picture. It's best not to post a profile picture that could be too sexy, revealing, or foolish. But in the end it's up to you.

Cryptic messages

We've all seen those status updates that read like a riddle. They are typically very poetic sounding, like the lyrics to a song. They are usually intended for just a few people. Most people get annoyed with these types of messages. It's best to send them to the intended audience.

Friend requests to strangers

You wouldn't go up to a stranger and tell them all of your personal business including where you work, your phone number, and other details about your life, right? That's what happens when you send a friend request to a random person just to get another "friend." This practice could cost you dearly.

In Washington State, a woman made the practice of "friending" random people, and it cost her big time. She posted on her wall that she was away on vacation in Hawaii for two weeks. Someone who she recently befriended on Facebook happened to be a career criminal. He and a buddy knew she was gone for two weeks and subsequently broke into her home and took everything. Only friend people who you have a valid reason to.

Calling in Sick

If you've called in sick for work, but really aren't sick, at least refrain from posting a status update until you're back at work. Multiple people have gotten fired by because they have posted things like "Crazy night out! I'm still hung over" or "Enjoying a nice day with the family at the beach" when their boss thought they were at home in bed with the flu.

Posting important news

Facebook is a great place to post exciting news, but if you do, remember to also call individuals. Think of it this way, how would you feel if you found out your brother was getting married in a Facebook post? It might be a little hurtful that you didn't call him, right? You also might be a little irritated if mom posted that granny passed away last night in her sleep in a FB post and didn't bother to tell you in person or on the phone. Either call those close to you before posting important news, or forgo the post altogether.

Game requests

You may love Farmville, but not everyone may share your passion. Sending game requests to your friends is one of the biggest Facebook faux pas ever. This has caused more Facebook rage than just about anything.

Internet marketing

Facebook is a social networking site designed to bring friends closer together, as well as make new friends. It's not a way for people to shove their MLM products down other people's throats. Marketing the occasional product is fine, but constantly trying to pitch products over Facebook will only cause people to unfriend you.

Overposting

The great thing about Facebook is that you can keep your friends updated on what's going on in your life. But they may not want to hear what you're doing every ten seconds. "Serial posters" have a tendency to write things like, "at the store..woop woop!" And then two minutes later, "Walking down the cereal aisle."

Facebook was never intended to be an avenue for people to have their own documentary. Your friends and family love you...just not that much.

"Spread the Word" posts

These are the Facebook equivalents of chain emails. No one really likes to receive messages that ask them to get involved in some cause or to post about a cause in their status. These messages typically come from overaggressive marketers or people that are trying to save the world via Facebook.

Facebook Lists

The great thing about Facebook is that it is constantly evolving. The Facebook team highly values user feedback and is constantly looking for ways to make the user experience better. As was mentioned earlier, one of the arguments about Facebook is that it is too public. To mitigate that problem, Facebook has created a list function as a way to manage your account. Lists work in two different ways: (1) they control what news you see about them and (2) lists control what you share with others based upon how well you know them.

In addition to being able to make custom lists, Facebook has three lists already created:

- Close Friends – you can add people to this list to see more of them in your newsfeed, so you get notified every time they post something. You can also turn off the extra notifications.

- Acquaintances – the acquaintances list is for people you know, but do not need to stay in close touch with. You will not see many status updates for people you put in this list. You can also exclude these people when you post something by using the audience selector option.
- Restricted – this list is for people who you have added, but don't want to share much with. Typical people on this list include your boss, co-workers, teachers, etc. People on your restricted list will only be able to see public content or content in which you have tagged them in.

You also have the option to create custom lists to organize Facebook friends as you choose. Your friends will not know if you have added them to a custom list, so you don't have to worry about hurt feelings.

Facebook has an extensive privacy tutorial located in the Facebook Help Center. Users can get to their privacy settings by clicking on the menu arrow at the top right corner of any Facebook page. Facebook allows people to share information with only certain individuals using the audience selector function. The audience selector gives you four options to choose from:

- Public – maximum number of people
- Friends and friends of friends
- Friends only
- Custom – specific groups or lists you've created

Facebook also allows you to control who can add you as a friend. The default setting is that anyone can send you a friend request. You can change this setting by going into the privacy setting section of your profile. Users also have the option to block people from sending you friend requests. The user is not informed that they have been blocked. Facebok users can also unfriend current people on their friend list. Users are not notified they have been "unfriended."

For people who want to address other's inappropriate behavior in person rather than doing things like unfriending them or blocking them, there is a certain way to handle the situation. First off, Facebook should not be used as a way to publicly criticize others. If you see some behavior that you feel is inappropriate, the best way to handle it is to contact that person off of Facebook or send them a private message that others cannot see.

Your Facebook page is ultimately your responsibility. That means you have the freedom to control what information you share. It is highly recommended that people who are applying for jobs or trying to get accepted into college do a thorough sweep of their Facebook page to check for things they may not want decision-makers to see.

Facebook has changed the way the world communicates so be sure to follow these etiquette rules in order to get the most out of this awesome tool.

Chapter 7: YouTube Etiquette

YouTube has become a global phenomenon ever since its inception. The site has over 48 hours of video posted to it every hour. Many people have found fame and fortune because of YouTube. It's also a great way to share homemade videos about your family, friends, and pretty much anything else you're into.

Spam

It seems that everyone on YouTube wants to be a superstar. The site has become flooded with people who use the video service as a platform to get their name out there. Most YouTube sensations like Justin Bieber went viral, which means their video became popular on its own because people actually liked the content. A lot of wannabe superstars are resorting to spamming other people's YouTube channels as well as posting about themselves on other people's videos. Rest assured that if you are super talented your video will be found out. Skip the annoying spam.

Insults

Take a quick glance at most YouTube video comments and you'll see that much of them end up resorting in a profanity laden tirade against the video or another commenter. The internet, in particular YouTube, is full of "internet gangsters" who enjoy insulting and threatening others from the comfort of their mother's basement. Insults can be tied back to your account. If you happen to threaten someone, it could be used to get you into trouble with the law. And just like other things you write on the internet, they are written in ink not pencil – that means they never go away and could come back to haunt you. Plus, it's just plain rude to insult someone.

Videos of Yourself

YouTube is filled with videos of people making complete fools of themselves. It's fun to watch and laugh at those videos unless you are that person. YouTube videos can be watched by everyone so be careful about what you post. For example, you might not want to record and post the video of yourself slamming 10 beers in 5 minutes. It may be very funny, but you should reserve it for some laughs between you and your buddies. You never know just who might stumble upon your video.

Video of Others

This is similar to the Facebook tagging rule. It's very bad etiquette to post a video of someone that may not want to be on the internet. We've seen many examples of this throughout the years, and they have made for great fodder on video shows. Perhaps the most infamous example was David Hasselhoff's young daughter posting his drunken stupor. In this case, it was a young girl crying out for her father to get help, but in most cases it's just some friends playing a cruel joke.

Making Video Comments

What makes sites like YouTube so great is the aspect of user involvement. People can give a thumps up or down, as well as post specific comments. No one said you can't post negative comments about someone's video, but you should do it in good taste. In other words, keep your comments related to the video without insulting the person who uploaded it. It's also very tacky to use profane language when commenting on a video. Never make rude or insulting comments about the person's family, children, or pets.

If you don't like the video you should give a stated, but respectful reason why. Otherwise you should use the thumbs down button – that's what it's there for. Also, when making comments use proper grammar and spelling. YouTube is full of teenagers and kids who would probably have a hard time spelling their own name. Show you're above the crowd by using some decent grammar and spelling.

Publicity hound

There are legitimate ways to get traffic to your YouTube video or channel. The worst way is to sound like you are begging for people to "come check out my video plllleeeaaassseeee." If you must, just make a friendly comment about the video and leave a link to yours. Shameless plugs are also bad etiquette.

Comments should be short

Also, when you comment do not write an entire thesis. By nature, a comment is a short line or two, such as, "great video! Your dog is so cute!" Not a comment where you tell the entire story from start to finish how you grew up with a dog just like the one in the video. Keep comments short and to the point.

Chapter 8: Twitter Etiquette

Online etiquette is pretty much common sense type stuff that your mother told you growing up. Such is the case with Twitter. The social networking/microblogging service was launched in July of 2006 after being founded by Jack Dorsey. It is a widely popular service that allows users to make posts of up to 140 characters. Posts are known as "tweets." As of 2011, Twitter has over 300 million users. It's often called the SMS of the web.

Give credit where credit is due

Twitter is full of great one-liners full of wisdom and humor. If you decide to retweet someone else's tweet then you need to give them full credit. If you want to tweet something word for word then use the retweet function or put "RT" in your tweet. Don't be a tweet jacker! Some people use "via", but that is technically what you would put if you slightly change someone's tweet to make it your own.

Excessive self-promotion

It's perfectly fine to promote yourself or something you are affiliated with once in awhile, but it can become really "spammy" quite fast if that is all you do. That's a really quick way to lose followers and alienate yourself in the twitter universe. Probably not what you were shooting for while constantly promoting your product or service.

Link to your sources

Many people cite information from an article without linking to it. That is a twitter no-no. Also, if you link to an article one time then you do not have to keep doing it. Also, make the link shorter for twitter purposes.

Respond to your Twitter followers

It's common courtesy to respond to your twitter followers when they take the time to send you a private message or a reply. Some people have too many followers to do this to everyone, but you should take a little time to make personal responses. A lot of people only care about getting followers and could care less about what others tweet. You don't want to be that person. If you engage with people who follow you, it will result in better connections with your followers.

Reply or direct message

If someone sends you a direct message then direct message them back – don't reply. Chances are they direct messaged you for a reason and do not want the subject to be discussed openly. Some communication is meant for a public forum while other communication is best behind closed doors. For example, say you just got done with a job interview. It would be best to direct message them instead of an @ reply.
Headlines

If you put a direct headline on twitter then it's best to put it in quotes. You should also cite the source. For example: Sports Illustrated: "Tim Tebow keeps on winning. Is He the Future for the Broncos?"

Follow people for a reason other than getting more followers

It's certainly bad twitter etiquette to follow anyone and everyone just to get followers for yourself. Twitter is different than Facebook. It is a way to connect people who have common interests – it's more about the shared information, not the friendships. Facebook is more about the friendships. To get the most out of twitter, follow those who add value to you.

Hashtag overkill

Hashtags (#) are used to help people find tweets that are on a certain topic. Some people use them too much because they think it will get them more exposure. That is not true, plus it makes the tweet hard to read.

Off limit tweet topics

Twitter is a great way to express yourself, but avoid tweeting things that are racist, hateful, overly sexual, or divisive.

Twitter etiquette for Businesses

Many businesses are now using twitter as a way to convey information to customers, expand their market share, and connect with customers. Using twitter can boost your business if used correctly, but it can also alienate you from customers and tarnish your reputation if used wrong.

Businesses that tweet need to provide value to their customers or potential customers. That means being careful not to over promote the business, products, or services. People will just tune out or get irritated.

One great way for businesses to tweet is to share useful information relevant to your customer base. For example, if you own a landscaping company, instead of always talking about your prices and services, share some useful information about lawn care tips. This will make you look like a subject matter expert and will keep your tweets from being boring.

Chapter 9: eBay Feedback Etiquette

eBay was founded in 1995 and is a multibillion dollar corporation with offices in over 30 countries. The company was founded by Pierre Omidyar in San Jose, CA. The company was originally known as AuctionWeb before changing its name to eBay in 1997.

The rumor that eBay was started as a way for Omidyar to help his fiancée trade Pez dispensers is not true. That rumor was started by a PR rep, and was confirmed by eBay.

Millions of people use eBay every day and are familiar with the feedback rating system. Purchasers and buyers can leave feedback about their transaction, but it is often abused to the detriment of one or both parties. Here are some etiquette guidelines when leaving negative feedback on eBay.

Don't leave negative feedback out of emotion

Remember that many people earn a living on eBay selling merchandise. Leaving negative feedback can seriously tarnish the seller's reputation and business. It can even get them suspended from using eBay. The vast majority of sellers want to make an honest living selling their goods to customers at fair market price.

If something goes wrong, contact the seller directly instead of trying to get your problem resolved by leaving them negative feedback. Chances are the problem is completely explainable, and the seller will do whatever they can to make the transaction right.

Contact seller first

If you had a problem with a purchase in a store, chances are you would try and resolve the problem by contacting the store directly. The same process should be done with eBay purchases. You will have a much better chance at getting what you want out of the deal by contacting the seller with a private message. Negative feedback should be a last resort. It is used to protect the buyer, not held over the seller's head as a manipulative tool.

Go through proper channels first

eBay has several buyer protection mechanisms in place to ensure people do not get ripped off. They also highly scrutinize sellers, and will ban those few who do not follow the eBay selling rules. That means what you have is a community of honest sellers and buyers who just want everything to go smoothly. Should something go wrong with your transaction you should contact eBay support and the seller before leaving negative feedback. Only after you have exhausted all means should you then leave negative feedback.

How to leave negative feedback

People who leave negative feedback out of emotion often leave inflammatory remarks about the seller such as "This seller sucks! Buyer beware!" Feedback is designed to educate other users. That means the feedback should be professional and detailed. For example, "Seller took five days to ship product and never returned messages." That sort of feedback is helpful to other buyers.

Be fair

In 2007, eBay began using more detailed seller ratings across four categories. Buyers could rate sellers between 1-5 stars in each category. Buyers should do their best to be fair, and rate sellers accurately in each category.

Conclusion

Online communication has changed the way we interact and connect with others. It has also opened up the entire world allowing people who live across the globe from each other a chance to connect. The online communication platforms mentioned in this guide have deeply enriched all of our lives. We hope you have found this etiquette guide useful, and will implement the tips, strategies, do's and don'ts into your personal communication. New ways to communicate will come and go, but good old fashioned etiquette will always be around. We are confident your online communication will be enhanced and we hope you share your new etiquette tips with others.